SITTING
Like a
SAINT

Catholic Mindfulness for Kids

Dr. Gregory & Barbra Bottaro

Illustrated by Michael Corsini

WELLSPRING
North Palm Beach, Florida

Table of Contents:

Sometimes it's hard to slow down and just "be" where you are. It feels like there is always something to do or somewhere to go. Sometimes we have so many feelings: big feelings, powerful feelings, good feelings, or bad feelings. It may be hard to know what to do with all of those feelings. Taking time to just sit and be, right where you are, not trying to change anything, is important for everyone and will help you to recharge. When we sit and calm our minds and bodies, we are better able to be with our Lord who loves us and is there to protect us. Sometimes with all of the "doing" of our lives, it is easy to forget that God has a plan for us and is always there for us to talk to. These fun exercises will help you learn to relax your body and mind, help you control your actions when you have big feelings, and help you learn to just "be," remembering that the God who created the universe also created you and loves you very much.

Prayer of the Present Moment

O my God,
When I look into the future, I am frightened,
But why plunge into the future?
Only the present moment is precious to me,
As the future may never enter my soul at all.
It is no longer in my power to change, correct or add to the past;
For neither sages nor prophets could do that.
And so what the past has embraced I must entrust to God.
O present moment, you belong to me, whole and entire.
I desire to use you as best I can.
And although I am weak and small,
You grant me the grace of Your omnipotence.
And so, trusting in Your mercy,
I walk through life like a little child,
Offering You each day this heart
Burning with love for Your greater glory.

—St. Faustina Kowalska, *Diary: Divine Mercy in My Soul,*
  Notebook 1 (1)

St. Francis of Assisi
Feast Day: October 4
Patron Saint of Animals and Nature

A long time ago, St. Francis of Assisi was traveling through the small town of Gubbio, where a very mean wolf had been growling and snarling at the people of the village every day. St. Francis trusted God and knew that God would always help him, so he decided to talk to the wolf and ask him to calm down and stop pestering everyone in Gubbio. Making the Sign of the Cross, and with all of his trust in God, St. Francis calmed the wolf of Gubbio and made him promise not to bother the people anymore. You can become calm like the wolf of Gubbio, too!

The Wolf of Gubbio

Lie down on your back on the floor, on your bed, or couch. Rest your arms gently at your sides with your legs long and slightly apart. Take a deep breath in, and slowly let it out. Take another deep breath in, and scrunch up your face as hard as you can! Tighten your eyes, your forehead, your mouth, and your nose. Scrunch them all up just like a mean wolf!

Now let them out, and relax your face. Relax your eyes, your forehead, your mouth, and your nose.

Next, take another deep breath in and scrunch up your shoulders, arms, and fists as tightly as you can! Really scrunch them hard! When you can't scrunch them any more, let your breath out and let your body relax.

Next, scrunch up your tummy and legs. Tighten your tummy as much as you can, and scrunch your toes and your legs. Make sure you scrunch them tightly! Do it as hard as you can as you breathe in, and then relax your body again as you breathe out.

Gently shake out your body, and move your head gently side to side. Wiggle your fingers and toes slowly. Take three slow, deep breaths in and out.

What a relaxed wolf you are!

St. Francis, pray for us!

St. Simeon Stylites
Feast Day: January 5

St. Simeon Stylites loved God so much that all he wanted to do was sit and pray all day! So that he was able to pray without being disturbed, St. Simeon climbed up and sat on the top of a pillar for many years, just "being" with God. Even though the sun beat down on him, the rain pelted him, and the wind blew at him, St. Simeon still just sat.

The Pillar

You can learn to "just sit" too, even when you feel overwhelmed, anxious, or afraid. You can be strong and calm, unmovable, just like St. Simeon on the pillar. The more practice you have at just sitting, the better at it you'll get. This doesn't mean that you aren't allowed to move; it just means that when you do move, you're aware of what part of you is moving. This exercise is also helpful to do right before you say your prayers.

Sit down on the floor with your legs crossed, or sit up tall in a chair. Close your eyes if that feels comfortable to you.

Take a deep breath in through your nose, and slowly let it out through your nose.

Just focus on feeling the air go in and out of your nose.

Notice that your tummy rises when you breathe in and flattens when you breathe out.

Sometimes thoughts can come into your mind or feelings into your body that pelt you like the rain that hit St. Simeon. Sometimes you can get uncomfortable sitting, just like he did, and you'll feel like you want to get up and run around. St. Simeon teaches us, though, that you can learn to sit through these experiences without getting up, letting the thoughts and feelings come and go just like rain.

Take three more deep, slow breaths in through your nose and let them out.

You can do this anytime you need a quiet moment to "just sit."

St. Simeon Stylites, pray for us!

Blessed Solanus Casey

*"We must be faithful to the present moment or
we will frustrate the plan of God for our lives."*

Bl. Solanus Casey was a Capuchin friar who loved God very much, and God loved him too. God gave Bl. Solanus a special gift: the gift of taming angry bees just by speaking to them! Once, Bl. Solanus Casey saw a whole group of bees angrily buzzing around the hive. Because of the special gift God gave him, he knew there were two queen bees inside, and that was making the hive upset. He calmly reached his hand in and took out one of the queens, speaking softly to the other bees and calming them down.

Blessed Bee

Sometimes when we get caught up with the thoughts in our head, we can feel angry or out of control. Feeling angry is okay; we don't need to change the way we feel, but with practice we can help tame our actions, just like Bl. Solanus Casey's bees. Let's try this exercise to help bring our buzzing down!

Sit up tall, legs crossed or stretched out in front of you.

Take a deep breath in, and stretch your arms out over your head, clasp your hands together, and reach for the sky!

Slowly lower your arms while you breathe out and bend them in to make yourself bee wings.

Start to flap your bee wings slowly; imagine that you're looking for a delicious flower to land on. Start to take a deep breath in, and as you breathe out, make a slow, humming buzz sound.

Make your humming buzz sound last as long as you can!

Slowly, take another deep breath in, and buzz out your breath. Release your bee wings and take another long stretch up with your arms toward the sky.

You can do this anytime you feel anger creep up on you!

Bl. Solanus Casey, pray for us!

St. Teresa of Ávila
Feast Day: October 15
Patron Saint of Headaches

"From sour-faced saints, good Lord, deliver us."

St. Teresa of Ávila was a very holy nun in Spain. She loved God with her whole heart, and she wanted everyone to know the joy of being in the presence of the Lord. Sometimes she was annoyed or upset with her religious sisters and didn't want to be nice to them, but she knew God wanted her to be kind and charitable. Then God asked her to help make her religious community even better. Even though this was a very difficult process for her, and she had to overcome many challenges, she did it with a smile on her face because she trusted so much that God was taking care of her.

Sour-Faced Saints

Do you ever feel like you're missing your joy? Sometimes we get "stuck" feeling down because we're paying attention to all of the many thoughts in our heads, or maybe we are feeling disappointed about something or just not quite "right." This exercise will help you focus on where you are right here, right now: safe and loved. You can do this anytime you're feeling a little out of sorts, remembering that God loves you and is so happy that you exist.

Sit up tall, take a deep breath in, and let it out slowly.

Now, make a sour face—I know you can!—like you just bit into the biggest, most sour lemon you can imagine. Wow, that is so sour!

Now, take a long breath in, and as you breathe out, open your mouth and wiggle your jaw and your tongue, getting all of that sour taste out. Yuck!

Take another long breath in and wiggle, wiggle, wiggle!

Take one more long breath in and slowly let it out. Are you feeling much better now, or at least a little silly?

St. Teresa of Ávila, pray for us!

St. Joan of Arc
Feast Day: May 30
Patron Saint of Soldiers and France

"I am not afraid. I was born to do this!"

St. Joan of Arc was a young, French girl who listened obediently to God when he called her to protect her country of France. Though she was only sixteen years old, she fought bravely, knowing that she was doing God's will, and she saved France! Many people didn't believe that God would call her to such an amazing task, but she had so much trust in God that she was never afraid.

God's Soldier

Sometimes we might feel scared, or not up for a challenge, but remembering that God loves us and is here to protect us can help to calm our worried minds. You can be courageous in the face of a challenge too, just like St. Joan of Arc! Let's do an exercise now that will teach us to stand tall and proud, knowing that the God who made us will always take care of us.

Stand up tall with your feet slightly wider than your hips. Take a deep breath in while you raise your arms up to the sky.

Lower your arms as you breathe out, and rest your hands on your hips. Stand tall and proud like a brave soldier of God!

Now, imagine that the Lord is covering you in his love and protection. Imagine a soft, white, heavenly light coming down from above, covering you from your head all the way to your toes.

Imagine that this heavenly light is strong and warm, and it makes you feel safe. You can trust that God loves you and is here to take care of you, even when things seem big and scary.

Just rest here for a moment, knowing God is with you, all the time. Take another breath in and breathe out.

St. Joan of Arc, pray for us!

17

Bl. Pier Giorgio Frassati

"Toward the heights!"

Bl. Pier Giorgio Frassati was a very joyful young man who loved to serve the poor for the glory of God. He also liked to climb mountains, and he said that the higher he went, the less distraction he had, and the better he could hear the voice of God speaking to him. He was a very busy man, carrying out many tasks for his family and, at the same time, serving the needs of hundreds of poor people. At his funeral, his rich family and friends couldn't believe how many poor people loved him because of how much he helped them.

Verso L'Alto

Sometimes we can be distracted by all the things going on in our lives each day, and that may make it hard to hear the people who love us when they speak to us. We can use our imaginations to help us learn to focus on what is happening right now and remember that we can be in control of what we pay attention to, even with all the distractions in our lives.

Start by standing up tall and strong like a mountain. Take a big breath in, shrug your shoulders up to your ears, and as you breathe out, drop them back down.

Take another deep breath in and roll your neck from side to side, from front to back, and slowly in a big circle. Stand back up, tall and strong again, imagining the most beautiful mountain you have ever seen or can picture in your mind. We are going to climb that mountain!

Begin by raising your arms and legs up, grabbing and marching while you "climb" the mountain where you are standing. Keep going, all the way to the top!

Leave all your problems at the bottom of the mountain. As you climb, imagine them shrinking away in the distance behind you. Look ahead to the top of the mountain, where you will be so much closer to the presence of God.

When you reach the top of the mountain, take a big breath in, and slowly let it out. Smell the fresh air! How beautiful it is to be at the top of the mountain. Here you can think clearly, and you are not bothered by difficult thoughts and feelings. In fact, when you look down at where you left them, all you can see is the beauty of God's creation down below.

Take another long, deep breath in and breathe it out. Thank God for this day!

Bl. Pier Giorgio Frassati, pray for us!

19

The Prophet Elijah
Feast Day: July 20

Keep listening for the still small voice
If you are weary on life's road;
The Lord will make your heart rejoice
If you will let Him take your load.
—Hans Ernst Hess

In the Old Testament, there is a man named Elijah who was a prophet of God. Being a prophet means that God wanted Elijah to spread the Good News of his love for us. One day, Elijah was feeling really confused and disappointed. He went to the top of a mountain, called Mount Horeb, to speak to God, but he could not hear him speaking back. A mighty wind blew, but it was not God; an earthquake shook the mountain, but still it was not God; fire tore through the brush, but still Elijah could not hear the voice of God. Finally, when Elijah calmed his mind and just listened, he heard God speak to him in a "still small voice."

The Still Small Voice

Sometimes when we feel upset or our minds are racing, it might seem like things are worse than they actually are. Practicing mindful listening, like Elijah, will help you be aware of the present moment, so you can calm your mind and think more clearly, paying attention to the sounds around you.

Sit up tall or lie down on the floor, whichever feels more comfortable for you. Close your eyes and take three slow, deep breaths in and out.

Now, open your ears to hear all the sounds around you. Listen to the sounds in front of you, behind you, above you, and underneath you. What do you hear?

You might not hear all the sounds right away; some sounds you may have ignored before as background noise. Let all the sounds come to your attention. Strain your ears to hear every bit of sound coming into your ears.

How many sounds can you hear? What do you notice about these sounds?

Pause for a few moments and rest, just listening. Take three slow, deep breaths in, and slowly let them out.

Prophet Elijah, pray for us!

21

Pope St. John Paul II
Feast Day: October 22
Patron Saint of World Youth Day

*"Help us, Jesus, to understand that in order 'to do' in your Church . . .
we must first learn 'to be,' that is, to stay with you,
in your sweet company, in adoration."*

St. John Paul the Great was a beloved pope who was really great at just "being." Rising early each morning, he would spend a long time lying on the floor, praying with Jesus in adoration. Lying on his belly before the Blessed Sacrament, St. John Paul II was fully present in those moments with Jesus. He had the whole Church around the world to take care of, but by starting off each day in prayer, he found the energy and wisdom to do it greatly.

Have a Great Day

We can only imagine what his prayers were like, but we can use his example to help us collect our thoughts and feelings in much the same way. Let's start our day by calming our minds and bodies. That way, we are able to choose how we react today, instead of letting our thoughts and emotions take control of us.

Let's start by lying down on the floor on our stomach. Close your eyes if that feels comfortable, and then take a long breath in and slowly breathe out.

Take a moment to feel yourself resting on the floor in the presence of God. Just breathe calmly. First, feel the floor, then bring to mind God's presence with you here. God is always with you, even now, and always loves you.

Next, take a minute to think about how you want to be today.

You can think of a word to describe this: loving, helpful, thoughtful, cheerful, courageous, calm. Think of any good word you want to, and, if you'd like, you can say it out loud.

Take three slow breaths in and out. Rest here for a moment or two, just breathing normally.

You can ask God to help you make today happen just as you hope, and you can do your very best too! Have a great day!

St. John Paul II, pray for us!

St. Thérèse of Lisieux
Feast Day: October 1
Patron Saint of Missionaries

"If I did not simply live from one moment to the next, it would be impossible for me to keep my patience. I can see only the present. I forget the past, and I take good care not to think about the future. We get discouraged and feel despair because we brood about the past and the future. It is such a folly to pass one's time fretting, instead of resting quietly on the heart of Jesus."

St. Thérèse of Lisieux, also called the Little Flower, was a young Carmelite nun. Though she wanted to travel all over the world, she actually lived her religious life in a cloistered convent. This means that once she passed through the doors into the convent, she never left. Though St. Thérèse died at only twenty-four years old, her diary was made into a book that people all over the world have read! Despite living behind the cloister walls, St. Thérèse is one of the greatest missionaries of the Catholic Church! St. Thérèse did everything because of her love of God, and she promised to spend her time in heaven doing good on earth, interceding for people as much as she could.

Showering Roses

We can learn to love as St. Thérèse did. This exercise is about "showering roses"—praying for other people, even if they don't know it.

Sit up tall and take three slow, deep breaths in and out.

Think of someone you know that you'd really like to pray for. Maybe someone you know is sick or feeling down, or maybe it is someone you haven't seen in a while.

Think of something nice you'd like to say to them, and in your mind, or quietly out loud, say a prayer to God for that person. Maybe ask him to help them or let them know they are loved.

God loves us all as his sons and daughters, and he wants us to love all of his children as well. What a thoughtful thing to do!

St. Thérèse, pray for us!

25

St. Paul the Apostle
Feast Day: June 29
Patron Saint of Writers

Love is patient and kind; love is not jealous or boastful; it is not arrogant or rude. Love does not insist on its own way; it is not irritable or resentful; it does not rejoice at wrong, but rejoices in the right. Love bears all things, believes all things, hopes all things, endures all things.
—1 Corinthians 13:4-7

St. Paul was an early follower of Jesus, but he didn't start off that way. When Paul first heard people teaching about Jesus, he did not believe them, and he even tried to put them in jail! On his way to arrest the followers of Jesus, he was struck blind by God. When his sight was restored three days later, Paul really believed in Jesus and became a Christian, a follower of Jesus Christ. St. Paul became an apostle and a missionary, spreading the Good News of God's love all over the land, writing many letters about God. He even wrote some of the Bible!

Love Is Kind

We can spread God's love for us to other people, just like St. Paul, by doing good deeds.

Sit up tall and take a long breath in, then a long breath out. As you breathe out, let any bad feelings you have at the moment leave your body with the breath. Think of something nice you've done for someone else in the past. How did that make you feel?

Now, think of something you would like to do for someone soon. Maybe it's helping your brother pick up his toys, sharing your dessert with your sister, or asking your mom how you can help her. Breathe in and out slowly until someone comes to mind that you can do something nice for.

Pick someone in your life and show love by doing something kind for them today. You can practice these acts of love anytime you want; being kind will make you feel good too!

St. Paul, pray for us!

St. Faustina Kowalska
Feast Day: October 5
Patron Saint of Mercy

"Jesus, I trust in You."

St. Faustina is known as the patron saint of mercy. She became a nun at the age of twenty years old. When she was twenty-five years old, Jesus appeared to St. Faustina, and she could see him with her eyes! He wanted her to tell the whole world how much he loves us, and he showed her the love pouring from his heart. He asked her to have a painting of him made, with the words, "Jesus, I trust in you" written underneath the picture. Sometimes things happen, and we don't understand why. Jesus wanted all of us to know that he will take care of us, even if we don't understand, and that we can always trust in his love.

Divine Mercy

Sit with your legs crossed on the floor. Place one hand over your heart and one hand on your belly.

Take three slow, deep breaths in and out. Repeat to yourself, "I am loved, I am safe, I am at peace. Jesus, I trust in you."

Now think of someone you know and care about, and repeat: "This person is safe, this person is loved, this person is at peace. Jesus, help this person to trust in you."

Take a slow, deep breath in and breathe out.

Now think of someone you may not get along with very well, and repeat: "This person is safe, this person is loved, this person is at peace. Jesus, help this person to trust in you."

Recall these words, or repeat them to yourself, anytime you need a reminder that we are all beautiful and beloved children of God!

St. Faustina, pray for us!

St. Joseph
Feast Day: March 19
Patron Saint of Fathers and Families

"Let us allow ourselves to be infected by St. Joseph's silence!
We need it greatly, in a world that is often too noisy, that does not
favor meditation or listening to the voice of God."
—Pope Benedict XVI

St. Joseph was Mary's husband and Jesus' father here on earth. As the man of the house, he was given the great task of protecting Mary and Jesus. St. Joseph was also a carpenter—someone who uses wood to build things, like a table and chairs, or a crib for a baby. What important jobs St. Joseph had! To make sure he did his best, St. Joseph was often silent. This helped him to focus on each of his responsibilities and always be open to hear the voice of God in his heart so he could take care of his family.

Silent Pause

Sometimes when we are trusted with responsibilities, it is hard to stay focused on our tasks. Life can be so noisy and distracting! By taking a few quiet moments, we are able to calm our mind and body; we can focus on our tasks too, really being in the present moment, and maybe even enjoy our work!

Sit up tall in a chair or on the floor. Close your eyes if you'd like. Take three slow, deep breaths in and out.

Just focus on your breath and on your body sitting here in the presence of God.

Now start to notice your body. Notice how the floor or chair feels under your bottom. Notice the feeling of your legs either on the floor or on the chair. Notice the feeling of your hands either on your lap or at your sides.

Is your body warm? Cold?

Don't try to change anything; just sit with all of these sensations, paying attention to your whole body sitting here, breathing.

Don't try to change anything. Take a few more slow, deep breaths in and out. Feel awake and alert, right here, right now.

St. Joseph, pray for us!

Virgin Mary, Mother of God

"Let it be done unto me according to your word."

Mary was the mother of Jesus, and she is our true mother. God had a big plan for Mary, but it was going to be difficult. God sent the angel Gabriel to tell Mary his plan, and he told her not to be afraid. Mary knew that the path would be difficult, but she loved and trusted God very much. She said "yes" to God and decided to live out his plan no matter how hard it got.

Fiat

There may be times in your life, too, that seem difficult. Maybe it's getting hurt, or having to do something you don't want to do when you know it is the right thing to do. Sometimes in life we experience great difficulties. When Mary said "yes" to God's plan for her life, she knew that it would be hard, but she also knew that it was okay that it would be hard. Accepting these feelings can help us to get through tough times. God doesn't need us to be perfect; he only wants us to say "yes."

Sit up tall or lie down on the floor. Close your eyes if that is comfortable for you.

Take three deep breaths in, and let them out slowly. Feel your breath as it comes into your body and then leaves your body.

Think of a time when you had to do something you didn't like. How did this make you feel in your body? Where did you feel something unpleasant in your body? Can you feel that way now?

You can learn to pay attention to how your body feels when you don't like something. Think about where you are feeling the sensation in your body, and focus on it like an explorer. If you first agree that it is okay to feel this feeling, then you can start to explore how it feels.

Now, what is happening to the feeling? Is it getting stronger or going away? Feelings can come and go; they don't always stay the same.

> Take a deep breath, feeling it come into your belly, and then slowly breathe it out. Thank God for this quiet and peaceful moment.

Holy Mary, pray for us!

St. Padre Pio
Feast Day: September 23
Patron Saint of Stress Relief

"Pray, hope, and don't worry. Worry is useless; God is merciful and will hear your prayer."

St. Padre Pio was a Franciscan friar who trusted God and knew he would always take care of him. St. Pio was famous for saying, "Pray, hope, and don't worry," knowing that God has a plan for all of us, and that worrying is a waste of time. St. Pio went through many difficulties in his life, but his trust in God made him so holy that people came from all around the world to see him. St. Pio trusted God just like Jesus did, so much that he became just like Jesus. God worked many miracles through him, healing people of their sickness and even making the marks of the crucifixion show up on his body in something called the "stigmata."

Don't Worry About a Thing

We can help to calm our anxious thoughts and worries by recognizing how they make our bodies feel inside, not trying to change them but just letting them be. Sometimes we are worried about things that might happen in the future or even memories from the past. Thoughts about the past or future can sometimes make us feel anxious or scared.

Let's lie down on the floor with our hands resting softly on our bellies. Close your eyes if you want.

Take a long breath in through the nose and slowly let the air out. Feel your belly rise and fall. Do this three times, each time noticing your breath.

Now, let's take a deep breath in and imagine that our breath is moving all the way down to our toes and, on the out breath, all the way back up out of our nose again.

Feel any feelings you are feeling. Does your stomach feel like it has butterflies in it? Do you feel like your body is full of energy bouncing all around? Imagine that you are breathing into that part of your body and breathing back out from that part.

See if you can do that a few times, and if you want, just rest there until you feel like going on with the rest of your day.

Your body reminds you that you are in the present moment. When you focus on your body, you focus less on your worries. You can have peace knowing that God is in charge of everything, and there is nothing you have to worry about. Feeling your body is a good way to remind yourself that it's okay to be here in this moment.

St. Padre Pio, pray for us!

DEDICATION

To Elijah, Francesca, Gabriel, Avila, and Joseph—
may you always know that you are loved,
may you always know that you are safe,
and may you always be at peace.

Art Direction and Design by Madeline Harris
Illustration by Michael Corsini

ISBN: 978-163582-053-9 (hardcover)

Library of Congress Control Number: 2018949168

FIRST EDITION

10   9   8   7   6   5   4   3   2

Printed in the United States of America